Prayers to the Infinite

New Yoga Poems

By
Danna Faulds

Peaceable Kingdom Books
Greenville, Virginia

ISBN 978-0-9744106-3-0

Additional copies of this book, and all of the poetry
books by Danna Faulds are available by mail.
Send $15.00 (includes postage) to:
Danna Faulds
53 Penny Lane
Greenville VA 24440
The author may be reached by e-mail at
yogapoems@aol.com

Printed in the U.S.A. by
Morris Publishing
3212 East Highway 30
Kearney NE 68847
1-800-650-7888

This book is dedicated with gratitude
to my teachers in the Kripalu tradition:

To Yogi Amrit Desai, who brought these teachings
alive in me, and awakened a passion for practice
that still calls me forward.

To Lawrence Noyes, who opened the door of
surrender meditation, and whose presence
in my life is a blessing.

To Suzanne Selby Grenager, my first yoga teacher,
who introduced me to all of this.

To Yoganand, who has been unfailingly generous
with his vast experience of this path and its practices.

To Don Stapleton and Todd Norian for the
magic they created that long ago summer in
Kripalu Yoga Teacher Training.

And to my husband, Richard Faulds, who shares with
me the grand experiment of walking the Kripalu path.

Other Books by Danna Faulds

Go In and In: Poems From the Heart of Yoga (2002)

One Soul: More Poems From the Heart of Yoga (2003)

Sayings of Swami Kripalu: Inspiring Quotes From a Contemporary Yoga Master, Edited with Introduction and Commentary by Richard Faulds, Quotes Compiled by Danna Faulds (2004)

Introduction

When the title of this book came to me in the middle of a yoga pose some months ago, I was initially resistant. *Prayers to the Infinite* brought up too many issues, not the least of which was whether I was ready to go public with my private, devotional utterances. What is prayer? I asked myself. And what is "The Infinite" but a thinly disguised euphemism for God?

I had long since given up any rigid notion of an anthropomorphic, judging God, yet here I was contemplating a book that included some of my intimate dialogues with the Infinite. I didn't quite know what to make of this.

I knew, of course, that devotion has been a recognized path to realization for thousands of years, but prayer seemed to belong to another age. In a simpler time before science introduced its double-blind studies and skepticism became second nature, prayer might have made sense, but now?

I began to examine my own relationship to prayer and found there both fascination and embarrassment. Although praying had been part of my spiritual practice for a long time, I spoke to almost no one about it. I would readily admit to practicing yoga and meditation, but never said a word about prayer.

When devotional prayers began to find their way into my poetry, I was faced with a conundrum. Was I going to let my embarrassment hold me back from writing what was asking to be written? If I addressed these prayers to God, would I let anyone else read them? I eventually realized that my confusion and reluctance to own my prayer-poems, as I came to call them, was not only a barrier to the open flow of writing, but also to my relationship with the fluid and creative energy I call God, Spirit, Lord, the One, Beloved, the Infinite, or All That Is. Naming this energy, or trying to pin it down is problematic, yet the prayers and the poems that resulted from those experiences of prayer were clearly important to me.

Little by little I chipped away at this barrier. I began to write more freely and share select prayer-poems with my husband. Even with him, I kept my distance for a time, not talking openly about the inner life of heart-felt prayer that was blossoming for me, and keeping certain poems to myself. Gradually, as I shared a prayer-poem here and there with friends and found them well-received, I overcame my resistance to seeing myself as the devotional person I have always been.

I experience prayer as a two-way conversation with God. Prayers are my attempt to translate into words some of my deepest inner longings. They are an offering of passion, love, fear, anxiety, gratitude, or pain. Prayer is one way to connect with something bigger than myself, a doorway to an invisible realm.

When I say that my prayers are two-way conversations, I mean that I often "hear" responses with an inner ear. Sometimes I actually hear a flow of words. More commonly I feel a sense of peace, or harmony, or what I've come to think of as "Presence."

These responses are rarely dramatic. I've had no burning bushes in my yoga room, and no etched stone tablets have appeared in my lap. Yet I can't deny that something deeply meaningful happens when I pray. At times there is a subtle shift of mood from self-doubt to faith, or from fatigue to flowing energy. Prayer is not only what I say to God, but also an acknowledgement emanating from somewhere I can't see that assures me that my message has been received.

As the back and forth of this dialogue – God whispering to me, or me talking to God – began to appear regularly in my poetry, it was challenging to see the devotional side of me show up on paper. Coming out of the closet as a lover of God was confrontive. On the one hand, I was practicing yoga with the intention of experiencing non-dual awareness. On the other hand, I was speaking and writing prayers that clearly addressed God or the Infinite as separate from me, underlining the very duality I thought meditation, yoga, and other contemplative practices were designed to overcome.

These prayer-poems both captivated and confused me.

By looking closely at my prayer life, I uncovered a remarkable fact: the very act of addressing the Infinite opened me to a different experience of self and other, one in which I sensed divinity as an interior part of all things. Prayer opened a door to an upwelling of creative, healing energy, an indwelling presence. From the duality of prayer came non-dual experience, certainly not all the time, but regularly enough to catch my attention. When prayer didn't result in non-dual awareness, I often found a state of communion that was uplifting and soothing to my soul.

The experience of prayer that I gained through yoga and meditation was very different than what I learned growing up in the Episcopal Church. As a child, I mouthed the words to the Lord's Prayer without having a clue what I was saying. For years I confidently stated "Give us this day our staley bread," viewing prayer as a secret formula, an incantation to be memorized and repeated at the proper moment during the service. When I matured enough to understand that I could make up my own prayers, all I came up with were entreaties and bargains. "Let me do well on tomorrow's math test, and I'll put more of my allowance in the collection plate." Or, "Please let Aunt Mae get better and come home from the hospital." When Aunt Mae died, I didn't know quite what to make of it. Wasn't God listening?

The fertile years of the late 1960s helped broaden my view of prayer considerably. My older sister introduced me to the poetry of e.e. cummings, whose work included these lines:

> *i thank you God for most this amazing*
> *day: for the leaping greenly spirits of trees,*
> *and a blue true dream of sky; and for everything*
> *which is natural which is infinite which is yes...*

This was a prayer that had lost its institutional quality and taken on a much more personal tone. I soon discovered Emily Dickinson, and found that many of her poems had the feeling of prayers. Reading the introduction to a book of Rilke's poetry just recently, I was amazed to find that he actually referred to some of his own works as prayer-poems.

I don't know exactly when I made the leap from an intellectual understanding that prayer can be a deep and intimate communication with the Infinite, to actually having that experience. Prayer began occurring spontaneously and organically in the course of my yoga and meditation practice. Often these prayers would begin in a wordless way as a feeling of love, or longing, or an overwhelming sense of joy or gratitude that begged to be expressed.

I was heartened to find that Swami Kripalu, a yoga master and the inspiration behind Kripalu Yoga, prayed often and with great devotion. He advised others to pray at the beginning of their spiritual practice, saying, "pray freely and deeply, asking God to bless your practice." He further advised a prayer of thanksgiving to end practice, taking the opportunity to offer up to God your efforts to grow, and asking that they be consecrated and made holy.

Swami Kripalu wrote extensively about prayer:

> *Prayer is the first step on the path of yoga. Through loving prayer, the devotee gets very close to God. Where the boundary of prayer ends, the region of meditation begins.*
>
> *[The purpose of prayer is] to remember and regain union with God... Because the root of all unhappiness is a sense of separation from the Divine, prayers and remembrance of God always bring happiness, peace, and bliss...*
>
> *Prayers support the evolution of the individual.*
>
> *Prayer is an unfailing device for bringing introversion to the mind.*
>
> *If you want to go to the feet of the Lord, prayer is the supreme technique.*
>
> *Prayer is the silent speech of love.*

Putting Swami Kripalu's advice into practice, I began

to pray at the beginning and end of my morning yoga practice. I remember feeling self-conscious as my mind stammered and stuttered and had difficulty expressing itself. Over time, I grew considerably more free in my expression, sometimes using dance or other movement to give life to what I felt, and at other times trying to capture the raw feelings in words or written poems. These outpourings of the heart led me back to my own center, into the still place where I could deeply listen. Often my words were answered by what the Quakers call "the still, small voice." Inevitably, both my voice and the voice of this other found their way into my writing.

Sometimes my prayers seem like dry words spoken only by my mind. In those arid times, when I feel cut off from my heart for one reason or another, real prayer seems impossible. I discovered that there were aids to prayer. Uplifting or absorbing music is always a help. Looking at a statue or an inspiring photograph can sometimes focus my mind and inspire me to pray again. Just saying the words, "God, I give you this practice" can somehow open a door into a more spacious awareness by encouraging my surrender to the Infinite. One of the wonderful mysteries of prayer is that I never know when I begin which direction it will take me in. I only know that when I let prayer lead, I am the beneficiary.

I now find giving voice to prayer through poetry deeply fulfilling, even when I'm convinced I won't show the poems to another soul. Prayer has nurtured my faith, led me into profound moments of inner stillness and at times ushered me across the boundary to union. The simplest of my prayers, inspired by Swami Kripalu, is "God, I am yours."

What follows is an eclectic mix of prayer-poems and other poetry, most of which arose from my yoga practice over the course of the last year.

The poems have helped to shed light on my journey. May they do the same for you.

Danna Spitzform Faulds
November, 2004

Acknowledgements

Where would I be without the hundreds of yoga teachers who read my poems in their yoga classes, buy my books, write e-mails that bring tears to my eyes, and spread the light of yoga with selfless energy? I can't list all of you by name, but I do hold each of you in my heart with respect and gratitude.

A number of friends have offered particular support to my writing. I thank you for your kind words, your willingness to listen, and your e-mails and notes that always seemed to arrive when I was doubting myself or my abilities: Mary Ellen Curtin, Cathy Drew, Jackie Kaufman, Guy Kettelhack, Margaret Klapperich, and Kathy Kuser.

To friends and family who have offered love, understanding, and tangible support in many ways, I am deeply grateful: Stephen Cope, John and Kay Faulds, Martha Harris, Jayme Hummer, Lloyd Klapperich, Antoinette Marchand, Vandita Kate Marchesiello, Nancy Marcus, Adele and Justin Morreale, Len and Ling Poliandro, Marc and Meryl Rudin, Bill and Lila Schafer, Martha and Ralph Slotten, Hal Spitzform, Marianne Spitzform, Peter Spitzform, and Marc Paul Volavka.

And Richard my love, from the bottom of my heart, I thank you.

"As blood is to the body,
prayer is to the soul."

Mother Teresa

Take Me As Your Own

Lord, take me as your own. Let
your holy presence glow like fire
in my soul. Let me look to you
alone for my direction, your energy
coursing through me like the unseen
current of the universe. Consecrate
this practice, every act a prayer,
each moment released anew in
truth. Help me let go fully in the
river of your love, hopeless and
hopeful, shunning neither sun nor
shadow. May the whole of who and
what I am finally be revealed today.

This Surprising Truth

This I say from my dwelling
place within your heart:
Do not miss me in your focus
on transcendence. Look closely
at the world. I am the orange
glow of dawn, sun the color of
monk's robes shining equally
upon all beings. I am your
frustration as you seek me
and come up empty. I am the
dusty web you sweep down
from the ceiling, and the spider
who races into hiding when you
clean. I am disbelief, devotion,
grief, joy, and tearful entreaties.
I travel on the notes of wrens and
song sparrows just to set you free.
See each action as a bold attempt
to find me. Experience my reality
even once, and your life is changed,
rearranged, priorities shifting like
a lid has been lifted off a pot of
boiling liquid. I am the steam and
the source of heat. I am the soup
broth and the hand that grips the

spoon. I am midnight, noon, and every chime that rings to mark the time. And I say this – you are mine and I am yours. In this surprising truth, rest easy and assured.

Life Comes Calling

Life itself expands me
when I let it. I point
to my known edge and
say, "That's it. I can't
go past there. That's
my limit!" But of
course life comes
calling as it always
does, not respecting
borders, asking me to
stretch again, and then
still more, until I can't
even recognize who
I am. You know
how it is – challenge,
tragedy, grief or ecstasy;
where I am right now
just can't stay static –
the pull toward God
and evolution is too
strong. When I let go,
when I allow life in,
I grow before I even
notice what is happening.

The Essence of My Practice

My practice moves from edge to edge,
exploring the limits of a stretch, the
inner realm of energy and breath. Each
movement plumbs new depths of
self-awareness. Who am I now, and
now, and now? Who holds this pose
with single-pointed focus, or loses
the thread of breath and stops to
find the center once again? Have I
reached my full expression, or is
there another defensive layer I can
shed? When I align my inner
compass to the truth, the essence
that I choose is self-acceptance,
coming home again and again
to the energy that bears me up
each time that I let go.

Centering

Here. Right here, right now,
bring your mind to this place
and time. Invite it, even if it
resists, to sit and witness
what it is to be alive. Let
there be no ulterior motive
in this moment but to be.

Rest on the waves of breath
and choose to experience
all of it. Let thoughts float
through and leave again, as
the mind slowly settles like
snow inside a shaken
paperweight.

This is all there is. Here.
Right here and now.

Honeysuckle Season

Honeysuckle season – reason enough
to rise from sleep and breathe in
morning sweetness. The breeze
brings other gifts – a hint of wild
roses, irises, pine pollen floating like
yellow mist. I know the sun's dry
heat and the cool, damp silence of the
woods. I could die right now with
no regret, wrapped in morning scents,
held within a vast and peaceful presence.
I can also live until my days are spent
giving freely of the bounty I receive,
awakening, awakening, awakening
again to the intimate miracles of spirit.

Low Point

I've hit a low point.
In a succession of
peaks and valleys,
this is a trough. It's
dark as a nightmare
in here, and every
fiber of my being
wants to rise and fly
away, not stay and
face the bleakness.

But the moment I
resolve to be present
and not flee, there's a
slight shift in my
experience. I breathe
into my belief that I'll
always feel like this,
and of course I'm
different in that instant.

"Stay with it," something
whispers, so I do, watching
as the contour of the pain
changes, moves and shape-
shifts. I'm part of a
continuum, and when I

stop resisting I flow with
a natural procession of
highs and lows. It's only
my refusal to let life unfold
exactly as it is that leaves
me feeling hopeless and
imprisoned.

The Fire of My Longing

Lord, let me slip inside your
consciousness where only love
exists. Captivated by the flow
of energy, let me break free of
my restraints to reunite with
you again. I pray this, consumed
by the creative awakening you
set in motion in my soul. Fueled
by my devotion, I pray this with
your name upon my lips and
your heart beating as my own.
I pray this as desire grows and
ebbs and shifts. I pray as the
rise and fall of breath creates
entrainment, as I dive and climb,
search depths and heights only
to find you hiding in plain sight,
here within the fire of my longing.

Practice

When I focus on the stretch of
limbs, alignment comes as
naturally as breathing. I hold,
sink deeper, pulse out and in,
move to my body's own music.
No part of me is left untouched.

I learn the secret language of
muscle and bone, hear the inner
wisdom that makes itself known
only when I listen closely.

The release from one held pose
can be as sweet as nectar on the
tongue when I take the time to
make this practice truly mine.

That's Where I'm Heading

You mean to say that I am
plugged into the same socket
as that electric blue sky, so
vibrant that I want to lose
myself in its azure height?

You mean that the same juice
that runs the universe flows
through me like a love song
or a bolt of lightning?

You mean life isn't about
being good or perfect or
virtuous, but daring to
freely follow energy?

Are you trying to say in your
slow and patient way that the
presence of God is everywhere –

That even as I bumble through
my life I have no reason to hide,
that I'm not a sinner, but a
conduit for light, that even
when I'm dull and uninspired,
the seeds of my awareness
are sprouting, even now?

How utterly audacious –
but I know you're right.
Holding back just leaves me
feeling less alive, while letting
go leads – well – I don't know
where it leads, but I know
that's where I'm heading.

Small Avalanche

From the very top of a white pine,
where an angel might sit to watch
the finches, the snow began to
slip. Responding to an upward
shift of two degrees, the call of
gravity or an errant breeze, a
small avalanche hit the branch
below, then kept going. It
gathered speed until it struck
the ground and exploded into
a plume of snow that startled
a flock of cardinals in a nearby
tree. They rose like holly berries
tossed into the sky, setting off
a second snow slide that caused
a crow to take flight from the
limb on which it had been
sitting, and that sent still more
snow groundward. And so the
small avalanches fell until a gust
of wind surprised the woods with
measured force blowing a white
cloud down through the pine
needles. The wind left the choke
cherry branches bare again to
receive the fine flakes of snow
still lingering in the updraft.

Opening For Grace

Lord, create in me the
opening for grace to enter
in, a moment of receptivity
in which the unexpected
can lead me in an entirely
different direction than
I've been heading. Help
me transform the way I
see myself, allowing a
new perspective to wash
me clean. Then, help me
drop any identity or view,
letting go of anything that
separates me from you.
Leaving words behind
may I hold to nothing, not
even prayer or the wish for
oneness. Sinking, rising,
being, just being, floating
in the ocean of infinity.

Sentence and Reprieve

I drag this crucifix through
the psyche's winding streets
and nail myself to the cross
pieces. The two beams –
self-judgment and self-doubt –
stretch me between my
perceived shortcomings and
fearful questions of my worth.
Dimly, as I sweat beneath an
unforgiving sun, I know that I
sentenced myself to this slow
death. No one else pointed a
finger in my direction. I
pierced my own side, and
chose the vinegar to drink.

In the time it takes to blink
back tears I realize that a
different choice than this is
possible, even now, even in
my fifties, even with my
youth long spent and mental
patterns firmly set. Sliding
down from the cross isn't
easy, but I succeed. I pick
splinters from my skin and
leave behind two empty
pieces of wood lashed with
the judgments I thought
would always bind me.
Walking back down the hill
without these burdens, I
am light as a love song.

Something To Give Back

Here is my deepest and
most pleasing secret: I have
something to give back
to the Creator. It is no
material thing, this offering,
but the emanation of my
being, a wordless rejoicing,
spirit giving back to spirit,
my life as heart-felt offering.

What I give is taken in with
such unquestioning acceptance,
a receptivity so vast that I
want to pour myself out until
nothing more of me is left, but
instead of being empty, again
and then again I overflow
with radiance and awe.

I thought I had to wrestle
what I needed from the
world, when really what I
wanted most was to give
myself to wholeness;
essence merged and
blending back again in an
unending circuit of energy.

This circular sacrament of
giving and receiving is
complete unto itself, a devotional
prayer in motion offered from
the chalice of my soul.

Release

The being of my being is released
from a dense and breathing body
to fly like a raven in the ether.

I live the simultaneous truth of
flesh and life force, irrepressible
freedom and mortality.

I am matter and energy, expressed and
inexpressible, deathless yet still moving
toward my last embodied breath.

The mystery of spirit leads me to the
four directions then back to center,
imbuing form with consciousness,
forging a sure link to my release.

Something far more vast than
individual identity witnesses all this.
The eye of my eye sees without the

veil of memory. The ear of my ear
hears outside the envelope of time-
bound sounds. The heart of my heart

wraps itself around polarities; unity
and uniqueness both embraced with
equal pleasure.

Everywhere You Think I'm Not

Although I welcome all of your
attempts, and bless your good
intentions, you don't need to try
so hard to reach me. I'm right
here – near as the iris to the eye,
the marrow to the bone. Your
will and my own do not live in
opposition, but coincide, mingle,
evolve from the intimacy of
giving and receiving love.

Does it seem audacious to
believe you give love to the
Sacred? In fact it is audacity
to think yourself so separate and
distinct that your link to what is
true is broken or obscured. Life
is not a game where I hide and
you grovel, beg, and plead to
find me. I am the very ground
of your being. I await you, not
only in the center of your heart,
but everywhere you think I'm not.

I Give You the Silence

Lord, I give you body, mind,
and breath. I give you my
geographical preferences, my
survival fears, my worries over
money, livelihood, calling, faith
and fame. I give you my pain
and weakness, and also my
strength. I give you all the
ingredients from which I
concoct the myth of separation.

I give you words, and poems and
personal stories. I give you my
end and beginning, and most
especially the middle, where I
feel most stuck, suspended like
a cloud floating nowhere in
particular when I'd rather be an
arrow aimed straight at revelation.

I give you my concept of truth and
illusion, and all my clever metaphors.
What's left? I give you emptiness
and joy, grief at goings and comings
and seasons. I give you my prayers
along with my uneasiness, my certainty
that you are listening, and my doubt.

I give you my hope that I can influence
any outcome. Finally, I give you my
giving. Growing silent at last,
I give you the silence.

The Inner Nature of the World

The night's depth draws from me
this truth: It's not my obedience
that is useful to the universe, but
my freedom. It's not compliance
and passivity that feeds the infinite,
but passion, conscious action, the
magnetic attraction and repulsion
of desire seen through clear eyes.

If I am scared and mute I lose the
opportunity to see the inner nature
of the world revealed as awareness
and energy. Only by betting on
myself can I live the full expression
of singularity and oneness. Only by
daring to be free can I live into my
awakening.

Closed Fist or Open Hand

I've always taken a tight-
fisted approach to life,
clutching at my suffering
as if nothing else exists but
this worry, doubt, confusion
or despair. I held my misery
close because it was known,
instead of risking the void
by letting go.

Now I try opening my hand,
feeling the stiff fingers peel
back one by one, to leave my
palm flat, like a launch pad.

Relaxing that tight grip feels
impossible until I do it, and
then I'm left shaking my head
in disbelief. What exactly
did I think I had to grasp?

Nowhere to Hide

Help me stay awake to every moment
of this day – the events I like and those
I don't – equally welcomed in my sight,
or at least not pushed away. Help me
celebrate the simple truths, the march
of clouds across blue sky, the scent of
purple hyacinths, the small green pea
shoots pushing up from seeds. If I am
made in your image and likeness, may
my heart grow wider and wider until
nothing in this world is left outside,
and I have nowhere to hide from love.

Transience

A moving line of diamonds
follows the wave's advance
to dance like sprites at the
shoreline.

I stand at the boundary
between water and land, where
ocean transforms rock to
sand. Sea moves stones, carves
cliffs and chooses inlets.

What seems permanent
changes over eons and ages
to prove the truth
of transience.

One And Two Are Both True

"I am everywhere present," said
the Lord. Seek me in the stately
trees or the melodies of sparrows
and you will surely find me.
Look for me in the Buddha's
smile, the countenance of Christ,
the words of the Koran and Sanskrit
prayers. I am always there. Turn
your attention to the sky where the
movements of moon and stars trace
my beauty. Experience true emptiness
and my presence permeates the
void. Now bring your focus closer
to your heart. Grow still and find
me within you. Separation
dissolves like salt in water when
you experience your true identity
as me. From knower and perceived,
seer and seen, from two comes One.
Practice devotion and let go into the
ocean of my love, or be the open space
from which all things arise. One
and two, duality and union, are both
true. So I say to you be jubilant,
and be at peace, for inside you is
the seed and fruit, the tree and root.
Choose to be in communion with
me and see the whole of this
creation infused with one energy.

The Next Moment

I wish to shed the skin
of understanding and
loosen the thread of
thoughts strung tightly
one by one like beads
on a choke collar.
I want the wild animal
of me to run free, the
passionate imagining
that needs no meaning.
I want to spin my fierce
wisdom into myth, a
gossamer web thin
enough to blow away
in just a hint of wind,
leaving my heart open
again for the next
moment of knowing.

Instructions

Hold the silence like
a mother holds her child.

Hold your ground while
all around you structures
crumble into nothing.

Focus on the still point
in your center until you
are filled with light, until

Spirit speaks to you in
words you understand,
until the love in your

heart grows so strong
it must be shared.

Tree of Life

I am the immoveable root
of a tree I can't see, whose
trunk and branches extend
up and out to an infinity of
being, whose leaves catch
light and transform it into
energy. I feel the taproot
running deep, sustaining me.

Without it, I couldn't
bend in the wind or stand
through raging tempests.
It extends down and in,
anchor and liberator,
reaching back to the
primordial sea of love,
connecting me with the
unseen in all directions.

My fruit falls far beyond
my reach, and the seeds
are scattered far and wide.
A few are planted by wise
hands in fertile soil, and
grow – even though
I don't know where.

Consecrate My Practice

Lord, I ask you to
consecrate my practice
so it becomes not just
disparate acts that I'm
performing, but sacraments.

Teach me the true meaning
of surrendering to you,
willingly giving up my
view of who I am that you
may work through me for
the greater good.

Grant me the strength to
see past my habitual ways
of being, that I may give
back the full spectrum of
my gifts and contributions,

holding back nothing,
releasing into the stream
of energy and awareness,
living the whole truth
and nothing but the truth.
Amen.

Outside the Thinking Mind

I find sustenance outside
the thinking mind.

As the thought stream quiets,
awareness comes to focus on
a single point, then moves –
shooting through me like the
light from distant stars.

Focus follows energy, rides
like a feather on the breath,
flies to the source of ecstasy
and life force.

Focus carries me everywhere
and nowhere, flowing like
water in a fountain.

Is it any wonder I return,
morning after morning,
to the still point at
the heart of motion?

Resistance

I am a bundle of resistance.
Nothing tempts me beyond
my insistence on being
miserable. The birdfeeder
is empty and the ten steps
required to fill it appear like
an enormous expenditure of
energy. I do it, one scoop in
the feeder, and some seeds
scattered on the platform at
the corner of the deck. There.
That's done. I'm finished.

But something tells me to put
out a handful of the special seed
the doves and juncos like. I don't
want to. More steps, more energy
expended. An image of doves
flashes through my mind and
I think, "I'll do it for the doves."
I plunge my hand into the metal
can and fling the seed onto the
platform. Okay. That's it.

As I trudge slowly up the stairs
beneath the cloud of my dark
mood, I see two doves already
pecking up the seeds. The birds
are pearl gray, delicate and
handsome, and despite myself
I grin. The weight of my
resistance lifts, if only
for a while.

Taking Refuge

I take refuge in the One.
The sole source and
unifying force is where
I draw my sustenance.

I take refuge in what is,
not necessarily liking it,
but awake, alive, and vibrant
in the face of what is real.

I take refuge in the energy
that flows from somewhere
I can't see to shape reality
like a potter molds her clay.

To those who opened doors
and walked before me on this
path I have deep gratitude, but
it's in Truth that I take refuge.

Simple Gratitude

A flock of robins dart from worm to
worm, drunk on the bounty of the morning
hunt. One robin stops mid-stride, a piece
of worm still wriggling in her beak. Her
eyes blink twice as she looks skyward,
pauses, as if listening, then trills a tune
so cheerful it lifts the gloom and fills
the world with simple gratitude. I ride
that wave of birdsong into dawn.

No Separate Thread

The ordinary and the unified field
don't just co-exist, they coincide in
the same place, at the same time.
Divine and human can't be teased
apart – there is no separate thread
to pull heart from mind or soul.

There is only the unbroken chain of
wholeness forged link by link in a
continuum. What is sacred and awake
is inextricably braided into the everyday,
but we forget that we can't dissect the
mundane from the radiant.

We lose ourselves in the rush to get
things done. Our memory grows dim
and there is such longing. We desperately
seek something, anything, to plug us back
into what we've always been, forgetting
that the disconnect is only an illusion,
easily erased in the choice to see the truth.

Communion With What Is

Lord, I am an ordinary seeker,
searching for relief from pain.
I have little to offer but my love,
and the blood that pulses like a
drumbeat, urging me to stay the
course despite the doubts that
bind me like a ball and chain.
I lay my day at your feet praying
for purpose and for meaning,
praying that you weave me into
the fabric of your waking dreams
so I am always one with your
reality. I offer you the wreckage
of my expectations, the shards of
my philosophies and "isms."
I offer my devotion, playing out in
stillness and in motion, uncertain
or sure, depending on the moment.
I pray for strength, that I may enter
intimate communion with what is.

Opportunities

When four wild turkeys
burst from a drainage
ditch to race across a
field, that could have
been enough. Or
the rainbow cloud, a
diffuse prism in midair,
or the ribbon of stars
in the Milky Way on
a clear night. Moments
like these are openings
for discovery and
remembrance; instances
when the veil between
the worlds grows thin
and there is a chance for
awakening. So many
opportunities to see
right through the
illusions that bind me

up in knots, to cut the
tangled rope without
untying, to pierce the
silence with a song of
such originality and
loveliness that a flock
of geese grow quiet,
just to hear, and the
prayer plant on the
window sill lifts
her leaves to listen.

Sunday Morning

I pray simply: "Take me,
please, that I might serve
Thee now and always."

In that instant, I am received
in the vast and beating
heart of God.

I am seen with all my
imperfections, personal
demons and attachments.

I am seen and received as if
I've always lived here, which
of course I have.

Opening my eyes, the same
trees are visible through the
same windows. The same
wood beams run across
the ceiling.

I could choose to forget –
it would be as easy as getting
up to make breakfast.

Or I can remember the undeniable
energy of love I felt for that brief
moment.

I can allow wonder to linger at
the edges of my mind like heat
lightning on a summer night,
illuminating the horizon.

We are capable of such love as
can eclipse all depravity and
fear. No, it's not that we are
capable of such love – we *are*
that infinite compassion.

It dwells in us and we in it.
Although we wander far afield,
it doesn't change the truth.

I close my eyes, and it is still
there, that moving, changing,
welcoming energy, always there,
patient, waiting, always waiting
for me to come again.

Easy

I sit until my mind slips
into silence, and in that
eclipse of thought, a drop
of nectar forms. I pierce
the perfect surface of this
drop and travel inward an
immeasurable distance –
it could be light years or
the smallest fraction of
an inch. I'm filled with
everything and nothing,
as I rest in the center of
this mystery, utterly
content. My striving
mind is spent, and in the
quiet I realize how simple
it is to arrive and taste the
sweetness – and how
easy to forget.

Unchained At Last

I lift the lid off my experience.
Instead of holding it at a
distance, I dive right in and
stare at my stale identity
without flinching. This isn't
me, or it's such a small part
as to be insignificant. I stop
trying to fit myself into
someone else's mold, and
let go of what I've known.

In that moment of surrender,
swirls of color glide and pirouette
behind closed eyes. My spirit flies
like a captive bird turned loose
into the open sky. Nothing can
contain me. I am unchained
at last, a torrent tumbling from a
hidden source, a flow undeterred
by boulders, holding to no form.
Finally, I know myself as energy.

Message In the Wind

The wind snatches a thought
from my head and makes off
with it before I can catch it
again. Of course, I don't
really try. Why would I,
thoughts being cheaper than
cow dung? But now the laces
of my mind come undone,
and I can't help myself –
I run barefoot in the snow
while my hair billows out
like a wild pony's mane.

"Here I am, take all of me," I
yell at the wind, who grabs the
words from my mouth and
howls in reply. "I really mean it!"
I shout. "Take me. Liberate me.
Sweep me away from my routines
and what I think I know about
the truth. When I wake up, let it
be to a whole new life, a new me,
no beliefs or preconceived
ideas to fetter creativity."

The wind roars but it ignores me.
Twigs, leaves, bits of ice, a piece
of plastic bag blow past while I

stand there, jumping from one
freezing foot to the other. Finally,
the wind dies down just long
enough to give me this advice:

"Go inside before you catch your
death," it says. "Go in and seek your
own road to liberation. Mine looks
like hurricanes and cooling summer
breezes. Mine takes the shape of
tornadoes and the lightest touch
of air moving across a bare breast.
Find your own way, and when
you do, pursue it with abandon."

So I go indoors, plunge my
frigid feet into a tub of the
hottest water I can stand and
feel like I've won the lottery, or
been to France. I feel like nothing
is the same, but it's still me I see
reflected in the mirror.

I dry my toes and dance with
such passion that I dissolve like
honey in hot tea and never
hear the wind whistle at me
as it rushes past the window.

Short Prayer of Thanks

Lord, thank you for this time
to be, to see, and live in harmony.
Thank you for sanctifying each
act and thought, for teaching me
that the heart's expansion and
contraction is just a natural
part of being human. Thank
you for accepting my many
imperfections hanging out
for all to see like laundry
on the line. Thank you for
showing me with such
equanimity that life is so
much wider than my mind.

Abide In Light

Abide in the quiet.
As the sun pours
new life into the sky,
and the birds sing
their morning prayers,
abide in your own
silence. The day
opens like a cathedral
door, and you are
blessed, poised at the
edge of this holiest of
moments. Sacred
presence consecrates
your every breath.
Abide in light, as if
you slip inside stained
glass, inviting all
of life to join you
in the quiet.

Inner Compass

My inner compass points
in only one direction. I'm
drawn, like moth to flame
by a force that doesn't fade
with time, but only grows
stronger. My desire for the
truth wrestles with fear
and wins, overcomes doubt,
gives up distractions one by
one so I can find my center.

I rest there then, if only for a
breath, suffused with energy
and contentment. The shackles
of self-judgment drop away.
The noose of my confusion slips
from my neck. I am changed in
in subtle and not so subtle ways,
as the experience of truth
sculpts me like clay in the
hands of the Creator.

What I Have To Give

How can I offer up to you what has
always been yours – this day, with
all my plans and aspirations, this
heart, sometimes closed, sometimes
so wide open the universe could hide
inside and still have room to grow?

What can I give you? Your energy
moves through me as a whisper or a
wave, and what started out as prayer
becomes a love song. I stop trying to
control and the moment I let go,
I dissolve in a sea of energy. This
bliss, this shift of consciousness,
my soul discovering that it is whole –
this is what I have to give.

Pairs of Opposites

I was born to bridge
the pairs of opposites,
to span the apparent
distance between light
and dark, joy and sorrow.

I exist to see past
differences, to open my
arms so wide that all
I can see and know and
be is inside my reach.

I am here to give and
receive love; so closely
attuned to All That Is
that breathing is an act
of passionate attraction.

I am not caught, but
freed by the seeming
contradictions between
seer and seen, knower
and known.

In the tidal ebb and flow
between lover and beloved
I explore the rugged
coastline of surrender.

Autumn Flight

A lone leaf cartwheels
skyward, riding an updraft
over the house, flying like
a drunken dove to the edge
of the far woods. What a
glorious end, to be borne
aloft, the whole Autumn
landscape spread out below
in riotous gold and orange;
nature caught in a flagrant
act of transformation.

Holding the Posture

I hold with focused breath,
heat radiating from a
firm intention to surrender.

I stretch, finding strength inside
my fear of failure. Body shakes,
then softens. Wild mind races
off on a blind ride and then
returns to inner sensations.

Breath pulses, prays, plays
through the center of the pose
and brings me – the willing,
willful, seeker, finder – brings
me to the beauty of my soul.

The Crows Know

The crows know it's all
right here – the clear, blue
sky, sunrise highlighting hills
decked out in autumn finery.

It would be easy to miss
them, sitting like sentinels
in the highest limbs, taking
in the scene's perfection.

They watch the river of mist
lift from the lake and slide
smoothly over stones and
fields 'til daylight burns it off.

As the crow flies, there is
no distance at all between
seeking and finding. Crows
know nothing's ever lost.

Two of them find their
voices at the same time,
proclaiming whatever crows
proclaim in the morning
after sunrise.

Making Peace With Pain

In the hour when night and morning
meet like the confluence of two
streams, I try to make peace with
pain. Behind closed eyes the jagged
teeth of a migraine chew through my
best defenses. When I stop trying to
push back I finally find a hint
of relaxation.

Pink fingers of light reach up the sky
from the eastern horizon. I observe
sensations shift and change, watching
how nothing, not even pain, stays the
same for very long.

The present reality of now is as
different from what came before
as season is from season. What I
believed I couldn't bear now seems
benign. I am exhausted and raw,
yet uplifted as if the hands of the
Most High have raised me like a
communion wafer.

Consecrated by pain, I am consumed
by the universe in the flames of
awakening. The moment shifts as I
listen to the waking calls of jays and
crows, feel the heaviness of sleepless
limbs, and know gratitude for all of this.

Prayer to the Infinite

Oh wild, unseen heart of light
and darkness. Oh spark of all
desire, consciousness, and life,
I pray to make this day sacred,
first to last, each act an adoration,
a celebration of what's true,
all of it consecrated to your vast,
unbridled exuberance.

I pray that I may serve by doing
what is mine to do, knowing
I will remember and forget,
find and lose, knowing too
that your infinite grace is
everywhere when I choose
to be attuned.

Expansion

I expand, expand, expand –
how can this be – yet I feel
it, my boundaries giving way
as energy and awareness
refuse to be contained.
Something nudges me to
leave behind my skin, like
a garter snake at molting
time. I expand, expand,
expand again until I am
profoundly disoriented.
What am I without the face
I've always worn, without
the skin that holds me in?
I gasp as the broad sky
meets my opened eyes and
then expand, expand, expand
again until the molecules
of me disperse between the
clouds – yet, strangely, also
coalesce where I am sitting.
The thin veil that separates
me from everything parts in
that instant, a pure and
simple gift of the Infinite.

When the Needle Breaks the Skin

Doesn't the choice come down to this –
to use each moment, no matter how
beautiful or challenging, as a means
to open? There is every reason in the
world to close down or careen like
a pinball from reaction to reaction,
hijacked by emotion, fear, or lack
of contact with reality. Life is so
generous in offering ways to let
it in. Each encounter, every act
and dream is a needle threaded
through with truth. Feeling the
pain of penetration as the needle
breaks the skin is all that's needed
for awakening.

Communing With Exuberance

I try to weed this riotous growth, this
uncontainable enthusiasm of greenery.
I pull out the dead leaves, scatter
columbine seeds, admire the lilies and
the coneflowers. I coax the garden
back inside its border of river rock, but
my success will be short-lived. The
nature spirits here have little patience
for my expectations. These plants never
vowed obedience to landscape plans.

They live to propagate and celebrate and
spill their abundance over the stone
walkway. "You may trim us back today,"
the flowers seem to say, "but chlorophyll
and life force will ultimately win out."
They bear me no enmity, and simply grin
as I pull on my gardening gloves stained
green from past attempts to tame them.
In truth I love this unruly tumble of
blooms, and my weeding is no more
than an excuse to commune
with their exuberance.

The Moment of Unmasking

Make it all holy, Lord, not just
my yoga practice, but my life.
May it all be perfect fuel for
the fire that burns away what
isn't true. May I draw nearer
to you day-by-day as layers
of shame are stripped away
and I am naked in your sight.
And may I dance then, as your
lover might, not hiding from
the light, but reveling in the
moment of unmasking.

Line In the Sand

Shall I draw a line
in the sand? Shall
I point and say I'll
go this far, but no
further? Shall I
approach the edge
and then retreat,
staying on the
familiar side of a
boundary I can't
quite define, but
sense when I draw
near the line?
Or shall I etch the
line lightly, and
let life erase it in
due time, like the
ephemeral streak of
a meteor, bright, then
fading, then gone
without a trace?

On Peter's Watch

I know my world of rowboats,
sails and fish nets. The waves
and breakers speak to me and I
can read the mood of unpredictable
lake breezes more easily than
people. This wind is different.
It is the fourth watch of the night
when a gust tugs at my cloak
as if it would rip my soul from
where I hold it close. There is
no light yet in the eastern sky
but I think I see Him extending
a hand toward me. I believe
the Master walks on the sea,
bids me come, asks me to do
something I know is impossible –
to walk as He does, not looking
down to see if my feet remain
above the surface of the waves.
I gather all my faith to do His
bidding, but then I waiver. Who
am I that he should offer miracles
to me? Past mistakes and miseries
pull me down like ankle weights
and I begin to drown in an ocean
of doubt. I cry out, gasping and
desperate with fear. "Lord, save
me!" I shout.

In that instant I am caught, lifted
to safety where I lay panting in
the bottom of the boat while the
wind dies down and the eyes of
my friends move between my
face and the Master's. It is true
that my faith failed me out there,
attempting a feat at which no
man could possibly succeed,
but I also remember the swell
of the waves as they bore me up.
I remember the wonder of those
few steps when everything I knew
came into question. If I close my
eyes, I can still feel the strong hand
reaching out and grasping
mine the moment I cried out.

Hitting Bottom

I find no peace in meditation,
no satisfaction in my practice.
Arms-length or a fraction of an
inch from truth, it seems I
cannot get there from here.
A maze of overwork, unclarity,
and pain leaves me drained
and disconnected, as if all
roads from this location
lead to nowhere.

I recall the precious memory
of presence and try to pray
but the words rattle in my
throat like pebbles thrown
down a dry well, bouncing
off stones, empty echoes
hitting bottom with a thud.

Bereft and rudderless,
I breathe into the dark places
and surrender my attempts,
trusting that in a blink, a breath,
a nanosecond, I may be filled to
overflowing once again.

Hidden In the Seed

Do not dig the seed out,
seeking roots. What's
been planted will bear
fruit. Be patient. Wait
through days of rain
and scorching sun.
Wait through times
when pain seems to be
all you are cultivating.

The small green shoot
will only come when
conditions are just right,
when there is enough
light but not so much
that new growth shrivels
in the sun. Rest and
patience sets the scene
for the miracle that's
hidden in the seed.

Offering

Lord, I offer you this body,
destined to die, but still
vital in the sunrise. I offer
you this mind, preoccupied
with survival, yet knowing
there is more. I give to you
my heart, longing to love
without conditions.

When I give you all of this,
what's left is radiant emptiness,
the stillness of surrender, the
bliss of being at the far edge
of consciousness with no
certainty except your presence.
I ask only that you make mine
a direct path to the peace
that passes understanding.

The Taste of Truth

For the moment, I've stopped struggling.
The undertow tugs at my clothes, and the
current takes me where it will. Surrender
sounds like defeat, but this tastes like
victory, the sweet release into something
open, empty, yet complete. My heart
speaks, instructing me to relinquish all
control. I close my eyes, and see myself
dissolving while remaining whole.
When, at last, I am delivered gasping to
the shore, I know it was the letting go
that brought me home. I was saved
not by my strength, but by daring to
be vulnerable and weightless, choosing
not to hold onto any of the debris that
floated past me. Truth tastes salty, like
tears, or the wind-whipped spray torn
from the froth of breakers. Truth tastes
like drowning, feels like being spit out
of the belly of the whale to stand inside
a larger footprint on the sand.

Toad

Toad hops across
the garden stones.
No goal exists except
to leap from shade to
sun, then under the
umbrella of the lilies.

Let Me Grow So Quiet

Let me grow so quiet inside
that I hear the private
conversations of crows as
they fly by my window.
Let me be so open that I see
with different eyes this world
born fresh again at dawn.
I wish to take none of this for
granted – not the miracle it is
to breathe, nor the wonder
that I can choose between
truth and a fearful view of life.
May wisdom and insight
guide me on my way today.
Amen.

Breathing In the Center

I breathe in the perfume
of peonies, hold for a
moment as the energy
grows, then breathe out
anxiety and doubt. I sway,
as if standing in the cradle
of the cosmos. I breathe
in star stuff, dust from
the feet of prophets, spray
from the primordial sea,
and release everything that
shackles me. I breathe in
healing energy until I rest
inside the circle of my being
and land precisely in the
center of my soul again.

Humbling

Looking closely at the contents of my
heart is humbling. I am easily distracted,
pulled this way or that by aversion and
attraction. I worry and complain.

While I derive much of my identity
from believing I am aimed at the
Sacred, I am mostly self-interested,
or focused on the status quo.

I want comfort more than God, security
more than truth. Honestly, I'd have to
say that my efforts at devotion
are just mediocre.

My longing for God isn't false, but it
gets lost in busyness, obscured by
expectations, papered over by
self-centeredness and fear.

Despite all this, only love flows back
to me from Spirit. I receive no commands
to change, no judgments, just an invitation to
draw near. My heart opens in humility.

Present With What Is

Even as I rest my attention
on the unwavering center,
I see that nothing stays the
same. The moment is
dynamic, changing.
When I try to frame it,
freeze it, pin it down,
I lose the fluidity of now.

My urge to grow nudges me
beyond my comfort zone.
In order to evolve, I enter
the unknown and become
mobile, mutable, versatile.

Evolution and perfection
coincide, inviting me to
expand my view until I
see two as one, and one
as the sum of every change
and circumstance. I savor
this gift of living fully
present with what is.

Be the Energy

Trust the energy that courses
through you. Trust - then take
surrender even deeper.
Be the energy.

Don't push anything away.
Follow each sensation back to
its source and focus your awareness
there. Be the ecstasy.

Be unafraid of consummate wonder.
Emerge so new, so vulnerable,
that you don't know
who you are.

Be the energy, and paradoxically,
be at peace. Dare to be your own
illumination, and blaze a trail across
the clear night sky like lightning.

The Way of Transformation

Do you seek me, yet expect to
stay unchanged? Do you look
for transformation and pray each
day for the seas to remain calm?
That is not the way. If you stir
up cosmic energies, if you wake
the sleeping snake, you will pay
for your audacity. There will
be times of bliss and quiet, but
there will also be earthquakes,
tornadoes, tidal waves that render
the old trail guides useless, even
in the high country. Playing it
safe will only serve to frustrate
you who hunger for the truth.
Speak your choice clearly. If you
choose to move ahead, stop at no
threat, hold no thread of nostalgia
or contentment. Break free of the
obstacles that limit your strength.
I await you just outside the gates,
just beyond the territory where
you feel safe. The source of
all you seek is before you now
if only you can see it.

Thanks Be

Thanks be to the One in form
and to the formless wonder.
Thanks be to the empty void
and to its overflowing energy.
Thanks be to truth in all the
ways it manifests. I offer up
the fruit of all I do, knowing
I am not the doer of these
deeds. The One that works
through me in ordinary and
extraordinary ways is what
I wish to shower now with
grateful phrases.

Carried By the River

I do not know how the witness
slips into absorption, but I notice
the shift.

There is no great effort, no prodding,
pushing, or squeezing myself into
some arcane philosophical belief.

Practice simply delivers me to the
river of flowing focus as easily as
breathing. Grounded in the senses,
I come alive inside.

Energy moves through until the
me of me is washed clean, and for an
instant I have no history or memory.

There is still an "I" to experience this,
but I am without a fixed identity.
Anything at all could be carried by
the river to this shore.

Insomniacs

A muscle in my back has
seized, so movement now is
agony. Breathing deeply
causes searing pain. In the
late night darkness lit only
by a partial moon flitting in
and out of clouds, a mockingbird
sings so loudly in the distance
that it wakes a goose on a
neighboring pond. The goose
lets loose with such agitated
cries and squawks that it rouses
a crow who calls half-heartedly
into the dark. All this ruckus
is punctuated by the far-off,
plaintive sound of a train
whistle and a motley crew
of barking dogs. Insomniacs,
one and all. "At least I'm in
good company," I think, as I
once again attempt to sleep.

Here I Am Again

Here I am again, Lord,
offering you the fruit of
all my actions. I do this
knowing you are the tree
on which the fruit grows
sweet and ripe. You are
the soil, roots, and limbs,
rainfall, sunlight, soft
night wind. I've come
to realize that my only
gift is the nectar of your
love, distilled, expressed,
and offered back through
all my acts, and simply
through my being.
What I give you now
is what you are

Being Human

Illness pulls the rug
out from under my
presumption of control.

The transitory nature of
everything I take for
granted stares back at me
through hollow eyes.

Can I bear the measure
of this pain, or has it
crossed the line –
and if it has, what then?

I find it humbling how
rarely I surrender to what is
before circumstances bring
me to my knees.

Soul-Knowing

Lord, my entire being breathes
inside your wide expanse. When
I release the need for words, it's
your silence that I settle into,
your quiet that pervades my heart
and mind. In prayer, I find you
everywhere, your love reaching
out to touch what I thought must
always be kept hidden. Above,
below, within, without, your
presence cleanses me of doubt,
fills me with the soul-knowing
that choosing to walk the path
of truth is all I ever want to do.

With You

Consort of clouds, beloved
of the flowers, no boundaries
confine my flight or wanderings.
Slipping through the cracks in
your armor, I am with you, calling
you to come forth and dance with
me in the downpour.

My energy spills out of you no
matter what your circumstance or
mood. Find me in joy or in the
darkness of your worst hours.
Welcome me. Throw your arms
wide and celebrate each time you
find my fragrance in the lilacs.

I am anywhere you focus your
awareness. Call on me, remembering
that you are essential to the universe,
your uniqueness no less precious than
the stars. If you forget, I'll remind you
with a whisper or a dream, or a touch
so soft you'll think a butterfly
just landed on your arm.

It's What We Are

Beneath the seething sea of
feelings, sense impressions,
thoughts and interactions
the ground of being rests.

Like bedrock on the ocean
floor, it forms a container
for the psyche. It's the source
of the "something more" we're
always looking for.

It's here, not somewhere different.
It's now, not tomorrow or next
year. Sinking into its support,
we find ourselves uplifted.

The ground of being isn't
a goal we need to seek –
in truth it's what we are.

Infused With You

Beloved, may your presence be
so clear to me that I stop seeking.
I want to worship you in everything
I do – movement and stillness,
speaking and listening, waking and
sleeping all infused with you, so life
itself becomes unceasing prayer.

May truth lead me from confusion,
and faith fill the space inside my
heart so fear can't gain a foothold.
When life doesn't unfold as I hoped,
help me let go of my old ways of
being so I can experience the
full force of your reality.

May I learn to love as you love,
see as you see, breathe as you
breathe, or at least not turn away
from today's difficulties.

Inner Light

The inner light is always with me.
When I slip beneath the agitated
surface of the mind, I find it,
like a fragment of the Big Bang,
still glowing. This energy doesn't
depend on health or strength
or even mental peace. It isn't a
product of belief, nor is it "me" in
any egocentric way of speaking.

The inner light is always there,
waiting to be felt and seen, waiting
for me to release it through my
choice to be still and recognize
its presence. The illumination
grows the more I let it go. Like
radiant heat it flows out of me,
flows from my whole being
without leaving me depleted.
We're all like this – whether we
know it yet or not – tiny stars,
glowing in the dark.

Dance Without Ceasing

Lord of Life, I pray you
rise from root to crown.
Prepare the way. Open me,
and sanctify my path with
fire and light. Allow the
energy of love to grow,
to flow in all directions at
once with no impediments.
Let me be the bridge between
earthly and sacred, the
ridgepole of the house that
must be torn down so I can
dance with you under the
wild sky without ceasing.

Resting In What Is

I rest in sacred presence,
not seeking meaning or
essence, just resting in
what is. The power of
this stuns me – to rest
awareness on the One
is like holding the sun
in my bare hands.
Instead of being burned
I feel a surge of energy.

Whenever I trace longing,
love or prayer back to its
first impulse, there it is,
inviting me to rest, filling
me with wholeness and
contentment as if the
sun has risen in my soul,
and nothing else exists
but this.

The Message

Here I am, Lord, thirsting
for your presence. I know
this makes no sense. It's
as if I stand next to a flowing
spring and long for water,
but I feel cut off. I try to
reach you, but there's a wall,
a veil, an abyss I fail to jump.
There's distance.

"It's not true," you whisper.
"Here I am, as near to you as
breath. I don't hide or require
you to jump through hoops
to earn my love with acts
of faith or desperation.
Here I am, residing in your
desire to find me. Receive
me, and I'm yours again."

Just For Now

Just for now, without
asking how, let yourself
sink into stillness. Just
for now, lay down the
weight you so patiently
bear upon your shoulders.
Feel the earth receive
you, and the infinite
expanse of sky grow even
wider as your awareness
reaches up to meet it.

Just for now, allow a wave
of breath to enliven your
experience. Breathe out
whatever blocks you from
the truth. Just for now, be
boundless, free, awakened
energy tingling in your
hands and feet. Drink in
the possibility of being
who and what you really are –
so fully alive that when you
open your eyes the world
looks different, newly born
and vibrant, just for now

Home

You've sought it everywhere,
but you're already there.
Home – the flowing river
of the heart. Love holding
you in close embrace. It's
not a place, but a state of
being, grace received and
offered back. Home – the
taste of truth and refuge.

Synapse in the Mind of God

In deep blue, dawn blue,
translucent blue, I lose
myself. I am a synapse
in the luminescent mind
of God. My heart-mind
opens wide as I slide
inside the light, sensing
the link from the center
of my being to the inner
core of everything.

I am one pearl on a string
of pearls extending nowhere,
everywhere; bare awareness
filled with breath. Energy
pulses, toes to crown, or
down from throat to loins,
and I am tingling, so alive
I ache, eons or one breath
away from consummation.

Index of Titles and First Lines

A Note About the Author

Danna Faulds is a practitioner and teacher of Kripalu Yoga. She writes:

At some point during or after meditation or yoga practice, something asks to be written. Usually poetry, occasionally prose, a phrase, stanza, or idea will appear that wasn't there before. Making myself available to receive these gifts is so important to me that I always keep a notebook and pen nearby as I practice. What I write each morning brings insight, new perspective, or a fresh way to see my life. All of the poems in this book came from such moments when I chose to be present to receive whatever was offered to me from the depths of the mystery.

A former librarian who worked in law school, college, and public libraries before turning to full-time writing, Danna lives with her husband Richard in the Shenandoah Valley of Virginia. Happily married for twenty years, they tend an organic vegetable garden, enjoy the birds and wildlife on their rural property, and host individuals and groups interested in the deeper practices of Kripalu Yoga.

Danna can be reached by e-mail at yogapoems@aol.com